Roof Watching

Roof Watching

Edmund W. Jupp

intellect™
Bristol, UK
Portland OR, USA

First Published in Paperback in UK in 2003 by
Intellect Books, PO Box 862, Bristol BS99 1DE, UK

First Published in USA in 2003 by
Intellect Books, ISBS, 920 NE 58th Ave. Suite 300, Portland, Oregon 97213-3786, USA

Consulting Editor: Masoud Yazdani
Production & Cover Design: Vishal Panjwani
Production Assistant: Peter Singh

A catalogue record for this book is available from the British Library

ISBN 1-84150-810-1

Printed and bound in Great Britain by Antony Rowe Ltd, Eastbourne.

Contents

Preface

Like others in the "Watching" series, this book is basically an invitation to look, perhaps a little more carefully, at the subject, which is, in this case, the top covering of buildings. Our eyes are set in our faces so that they look horizontally. Hence, in the ordinary way, people mostly look straight ahead, and don't look up as much as they might. If they did this too much they might not see objects at ground level, and so bump into things, of course; on the other hand, there is a good deal above eye level that is worth seeing.

It is true that, without looking up, you can see distant roof-lines and, when the buildings are lower, see the upper parts as well. It is possible, too, to get a good view from the upper stories of adjacent buildings. Aerial views are especially helpful, though detail is hard to pick out from even low altitudes, and aeroplanes move too fast. Slower machines, like airships, and balloons, give a better view, though perhaps this is an expensive way to look at a roof.

Field glasses and telescopes are not to be despised. Even a low-power pair of glasses can reveal some of the interesting detail in a distant roof. This can be useful, too, when looking at the inside of a high roof, such as that of a cathedral. So a low-power set of field-glasses can be helpful at times. However, they are by no means essential for satisfactory roof watching.

To get full pleasure from this interesting pursuit, we have to approach the subject with some knowledge. It would be a pity to miss any detail of the satisfaction of seeing and appreciating the fascinating world that sits above the supporting structures.

It is not only the outside of a roof that is of interest. Inside there are all sorts of intriguing things. If you hadn't thought much about it before, you may be surprised at what goes on inside the roof space, and what holds it all up. So, inside and outside, the roof is worth some attention, not only when complete, but during its construction, too. A building site can be worth a visit at any stage of the construction, particularly so when the roof is being built.

The variety of shapes, textures, and colours of the covering provides a fascinating display to delight the eye and enchant the enquiring mind. Knowing something of the "why" and the "how" can add much to the absorbing pastime of just looking at roofs.

Roof watching demands no special equipment, doesn't cost anything, and can provide a simple diversion or serious study: instruction, entertainment and enlightenment, all for nothing! Those who wish may, of course, paint, sketch, photograph or otherwise record what they see; but this is not an essential part of watching. It can be an occupation for the idler as much as for the energetic enthusiast.

Once one is bitten by the subject, it can be pursued in depth to the satisfaction of the watcher, in any part of the world, even in Arctic regions (though variety may be lacking in these latter parts). Wherever you go, you may find yourself glancing up more than before, once you know what to expect. Just remember to stop walking while you are doing so.

Although poor weather may deter you from going outside, a rain-washed roof can look extra attractive, and you can see how it deals with a downpour, all part of roof watching. Some revision questions have been slipped in here and there, for those who like to ensure that they have understood what they have read. They can be skipped at will, of course. I do hope that you will find much enjoyment in tilting back your head occasionally, and I wish you good watching.

E.W.J.

The Beginnings

A roof is defined in one dictionary as "the top covering of a building...a ceiling, the overhead structure of a vault, arch, cave, excavation, etc..." and so on. That is quite a lot, but it does seem to cover everything. For our purposes, we can think of a roof as simply some kind of protective lid.

Early man, (and woman too, I suppose,) dwelt in caves, or went into them to dodge heat, cold, rain or predators. All kinds of other animals did the same. So, effectively, the ceiling they saw when they looked up was the underside of a roof, perhaps the first kind. It offered shelter, and was usually substantial.

Caves were not always available. In some areas there weren't any cliffs or rocks; and, where there was a cliff, the face might be sheer, without a crack or hole into which one might pop out of the weather. Some caves were inaccessible, too, if they were high up, or choked with undergrowth when they were in a forest. Some might already contain residents of a hostile nature, not prepared to share their shelter. Poisonous snakes and spiders are not the best of bed-mates.

It wouldn't have taken long for an intelligent creature to spot a fallen tree leaning against a rock face, and to copy the idea with branches, so as to form an early lean-to shelter. The slope of that kind of roof would help to shed the rainwater falling on it. The draught through the ends might have been more than a little uncomfortable, I suppose, but that aspect was not the concern of the roof itself.

This draught business arises because the open ends of a covered area can give rise to what is known as the *Venturi effect*. This is an interesting thing that happens when a flow of air, or any other fluid, for that matter, enters a passage narrower than that of the preceding flow, upstream. As the passage narrows, the pressure drops, and the speed increases. So if you stand under a railway bridge, for example, you are effectively under a roof with open ends, and you will usually feel the draught, a distinctly faster flow than when standing outside in an open space.

For a convincing demonstration of the Venturi effect, you can see the fall in level of a stream as it pours through a narrow part of a water-course. Where the stream widens, the level recovers, and the water slows down again. More technically, the energy content is constant. The total energy is the sum of the kinetic and pressure energy. You need not bother with this, though. Just remember: whenever you squeeze a flow, it goes faster.

Some railway station platforms are notoriously draughty places for the same reason. In the days of steam, a good cleansing draught was helpful, but conditions have changed, and such windy sites are no longer desirable. A few partition walls, reaching part-way across the platform, would help to reduce this discomfort. On the other hand, the through draught is welcome in the summer, and it does help to freshen the air.

Coming back to our roof, the first type was almost certainly a lean-to; and these are still around, perhaps the easiest to construct. A few branches tilted against a convenient tree or rock, and some simple thatching with woven leaves and fronds, and there we have a sound roof.

We might have to fix it securely against high winds, but basically we have a shelter, a protection from the elements as substantial as we like to make it. This sort of thing is still made in jungles, and similar places. The modern camper, too, might use the idea occasionally.

The more permanent type of lean-to roof is more complicated than those early structures, and is to be found more often as an extension to an existing building. Sometimes it is some architectural quirk, rather than an essential of sound design. A lean-to roof doesn't have to be straight, of course. It can be arched in section, or curved in plan. Look out for them.

A lean-to construction is often used as an add-on to a small house, for a garage, or car-port. Walls or columns support the outer edge of the roof, and sometimes the roofing material is translucent, letting light through to the space beneath.

This kind of structure is often a way of foiling the planning regulations, to gain extra space for a small dwelling. If you look around, you may spot some erstwhile garages converted into extra living space.

We can imagine early mankind proceeding from the lean-to structure to a roof supported on struts or pillars. The lean-to can shed water because of the slope of the roof surface; so a supported roof that is flat has an obvious disadvantage. It would soon be clear that a roof needs a slope if rain is about. It might even have more than one slope. A central ridge would provide for two sloping surfaces, with little ado, though it would no longer be a lean-to.

In some parts of the world progress was made to a circular form of structure, with a conical roof, an excellent idea. These conical roofs are used with great effect, and have aesthetic appeal, too. In the tropics, the little thatched conical houses are charming. A faintly "native" effect is often achieved by using this style on the beaches, where tourists flock, to afford protection against the sun which they have come to seek.

In the less developed parts of the world the erection of a single-story conical building is simple, and rapidly achieved. Marking a circle on the ground with a pointed stick is child's play. You put in a central peg, and run a length of string or similar material outwards to a tracing stick. Then, keeping all things taut, you just run the tracer round and you have a circle on the ground. Using this as a guide, you put in some uprights, and weave a wall.

The materials are to hand, some reeds or leaves. The roof is popped on, and you have a firm comfortable little house in no time. Walls are not essential, though they do provide privacy, and protection from wind, sun and rain. Walls are effectively incorporated where the roof is run right down to ground level.

A sloping roof doesn't need to be solid. If the materials are laid properly, water from above can run down the twigs, leaves or grasses to the lower end without penetrating; this is the secret of good thatching. The steeper the slope, and the thicker the thatch, the more efficient the protection against rain. You won't see many thin, flat thatched roofs! Notice how thick and steep they are, and how cosy they look, and picturesque, too.

Reed for thatching is durable stuff, and in Britain the best reputedly comes from Norfolk. In other countries reed from particular areas is popular. Thatchers are proud folk, and like to make good job.

You may come across a thatched roof bearing a thatched bird at the ridge, a kind of trade mark or signature of the men who built the covering.

Finding the materials for shelter, on arid plains without trees, grass, or strong shrubs, would have been difficult Perhaps early man didn't hang about much on the plains because of this. If there are no trees and no caves, finding shelter is harder. A hole in the ground is one solution if the soil is suitable, and not liable to collapse. The ground above is then the roof. You'd have to be pretty tough to enjoy this, of course; but then, those ancients were tough. So you could almost say that the first roof was no roof at all, just the ground!

As the centuries wore on, ideas about a roof developed comparatively quickly. All kinds of materials were used for a covering against the weather. It took a long time, though, before we reached the stage where we could choose from a wide range of materials such as stone, slate, tile, felt, and so on.

Modern temporary shelters make good use of canvas and the new generation of plastics. Cunningly braced, these can be sturdy, and proof against gales, yet lightweight. It is possible that early man occasionally made use of animal skins, thrown over a branch, precursors of the modern tent; but this is pure speculation. In any case, a flexible covering requires such material to be laid sloping, to shed the water.

An animal skin has the advantage of many fine hairs, which can conduct the water down, and the hide is impervious (which is just as well for the animal, I suppose). The principal advantage of a flexible covering is that it is readily folded and stowed, and is portable. Modern synthetics have gladdened the hearts of many who need a light shelter that can be carried around. These new materials are strong and hard-wearing.

The heavier materials needed substantial support, of course, and the design of a roof demanded some knowledge of the theory of structures, and some mathematics, as well.

Well, mathematics came along in due course, to be the scourge of some schoolboys but the salvation of engineers and architects. Many whose names are now famous wrestled with the theories of structural design. We shall have something to say about these matters in later chapters.

Those who deal with the design of a roof nowadays require a good grounding in such subjects as Applied Mathematics, Theory of Structures, and Strength of Materials, and there is steady progress in all of these. The "beginnings" are a long way from what happens on a modern building site.

Of course, you can still put up a good useful roof without a knowledge of mathematics. It may use more material than one designed by an expert, but it should keep off the sun and the rain; and if it doesn't, you can pile on some more stuff till it is shady and waterproof. In places where suitable materials are plentiful, they can be used to excess, and over-design doesn't matter very much.

The beginnings, then, are a long way back in time, and we have certainly made great strides in our approach, and indeed the very concept of a roof. We demand much more of a roof nowadays, and have access to more facilities, different materials, and magic machinery. Yet the basics are still with us and will remain so. We can still look around and see some very basic examples of a roof.

You may find it of particular interest to see how the earlier shape of a tent has changed recently. A camping catalogue can provide you with some good ideas of the break away from the traditional ridge tent. Inflatable members, new plastics, polygonal forms, guy-less tents, new styles of marquees, all show how far things have moved in the last century.

Recall

1. What is the advantage of a sloping roof?

2. Name some ways of providing cover against weather.

3. What subjects would you study to help you to design a roof?

4. What is meant by the "Venturi effect"?

5. Why doesn't water penetrate a roof of straw?

6. How did early man manage to provide shelter in treeless plains?

7. What benefit is there in using a flexible roof material?

8. How does a flat roof suffer from its being flat?

9. Name some modern roofing materials.

10. Discuss the advantages of a conical structure.

The Flat Roof

At first thought, you might view the flat roof as the obvious choice, simple to design and build. Our ancient forebears might have thought so, too. When we use the words "flat" and "horizontal" we mean a surface conforming to the surface of the earth. So it is really curved; but the radius of curvature is so large, that for our purposes, we mean a level surface, on which a ball will remain stationary and not roll anywhere, unless disturbed.

The flat roof is a step away from the lean-to, and it demands support of some kind. Whereas the forces on the ends of a lean-to come from the horizontal and vertical forces of the supporting face and the ground, a flat roof demands poles, struts, columns or walls to hold it above the ground. The forces on the roof are vertical, tending to make the surface sag in the middle, so the roof itself has to be designed to cater for this sagging tendency.

In general, we may think of the roof as a load spread evenly across its length and breadth. This is known in the fields of engineering, architecture and building as a *uniformly distributed load* or *udl*. A udl imposes transverse forces tending to bend the surface, being greatest at the middle and least at the ends. If we draw a graph or diagram of this bending effect it is zero at the ends, and follows a beautiful curve called a "parabola". Whatever we use to carry this load has to take into account this variation across the span, if we are not to use too much material.

A flat roof can be thought of as consisting of three items, (i) the covering itself, (ii) the support for the covering, directly beneath it, and (iii) beams or girders to support the whole thing.

Flexible coverings, such as roofing felt, need sheets of chipboard, or other boarding, to prevent sagging between the rafters. In some cases, all three duties can be combined in one, by the use of corrugated sheeting of plastic or metal. So-called "corrugated iron" is often used. This is not iron, but steel, which is an alloy of iron. The sheets have been galvanised (i.e. zinc coated). The corrugations supply the required rigidity. Although steel has been used for a long time, the term "corrugated iron" is still used.

A most useful material, corrugated iron roofing may be seen all over the world. It usually corrodes fairly early in its life, and the warm tones of rust mellow the brash appearance of the new shiny sheet. It can be very attractive. If left untreated, it can develop holes; and if these occur in the troughs, they feed rainwater through to the space below. If you look carefully, you will notice that where it is nailed, the nails are driven through the ridges of the corrugations. Nail holes in the troughs just ask for trouble.

Clear plastic corrugated sheeting is often used, as it transmits light to the covered area. The same considerations apply, of course, to the fixing of these sheets. This is a cheap way of providing shelter, and is easy to erect.

For a small roof, a few beams laid across the walls or supporting frame can manage this without much complication. If you look inside a small garden shed you may see this. The supporting beams are normally more robust than would be required to provide resistance to bending alone. They have to supply rigidity, lacking in the covering. So you will find square-sectioned or rectangular timbers running across inside the roofing of small huts.

For larger spans, the supporting structure may consist of frames, girders, or beams of varying depth. These may be deeper in the middle, where the bending effect is greatest. A girder which varies in depth across the span can cost more than a uniform girder. For this reason many smaller spans are bridged by "off-the-shelf" lengths of standard design.

Girders in timber or metal have upper members taking compression, and lower members to cope with tension. In between are the bracing struts and ties. There are several standard designs, the most well-known of which is probably the Warren girder, which looks like a series of "W"s, joined at their tops and bottoms.

This design has the great merit of using members of equal length throughout. So one might pick up a bundle of pieces and build a Warren girder with little difficulty. Since a strut can usually take tension as well, one might even use identical pieces to make it, perhaps tubing or angle iron.

Using identical pieces would entail some members being over-designed, i.e. under-stressed. This is wasteful of material, but the simplicity of design and manufacture might offset this, and lead to an economical result. Structural engineers are not ones to waste the money of their clients.

More information about girders can be found in *Bridge Watching* in this series.

The struts or walls which support a flat roof must resist *sway*, i.e. the tendency to pivot about their base. In section, they act as columns, so need to be designed to avoid buckling. A cavity wall has less tendency to buckle, as the cross-section is more widely spread from the centre.

At or near the top of the supporting columns or walls, the load of the roof is transferred to pads, and the girders may be braced to the wall. Corbels are sometimes used to take the ends of the girders, or braces. We shall have more to say about these later.

The girders themselves can consist of frames, or trusses. In some cases simple beams may be used. In some older properties, a stout oak beam was a simple solution in many cases, often second-hand, recovered from an old building or a ship. For short spans, a light rolled steel section serves.

Another popular frame is the Pratt or N-girder. This consists of a number of rectangles, each diagonally braced, to form a series of "N"s.

Neither the Warren nor the Pratt girders need have parallel upper and lower members in general; but for a flat roof they are usually straight. These girders are usually of steel, but timber is suitable for such structural features.

If you look up at the underside of a flat roof supported by girders, you can often see how the roofing material is attached. Advantage is sometimes taken to hang electric wiring, and pipes carrying gas and water, along the girders.

Lighting fitments, too, can find a home there. Such items must be fitted with care, avoiding making holes that weaken the members. For this reason you will often see clips being used, specially designed to fit without the need for drilling holes. This applies, too, to the fixing of the roofing material to the girder.

Impermeable sheets of bitumastic material will be found on many small flat-roofed buildings, sometimes sprinkled with gravel, as a fire check. This is a cheap way of providing shelter, but it does call for replacement from time to time.

Rainwater puddles, and what they accumulate, can eat into the material as the years roll by. Flat felt roofing doesn't reckon to be everlasting.

How flat is "flat"? It is usually advisable to provide a fall, even though it be slight, rather than build the roof absolutely level. You may see how this is achieved in a nominally flat roof by examining the ends. If a gutter is fitted, this will, of course, be at the lower end of the roof. Small constructions like sheds and garages are most usually built like this.

For a very large flat roof, support may be augmented by columns, between the walls. Here again, an apparently "flat" roof may have a slight fall into guttering on these columns, draining into pipes which run down the columns, sometimes concealed within them.

In a dry climate, where rain is little or unknown, a flat roof presents no problem from the formation of puddles. Small structures are simple, and the covering may be of materials which are not in themselves impervious. The great advantage of this is usually offset by the possible depredations of destructive pests which eat the supports, and perhaps the roof too, even the people in them.

A flat roof is usually a covering for a small area, since the provision of adequate support for a large flat roof demands long, strong beams of adequate depth, or intermediate pillars.

The outer covering is often of bitumastic felt or other plastic material, supplied in rolls, with a sealant along the edges of adjacent pieces. It is not an ideal material, but is relatively cheap to buy and lay.

Looking up inside a flat-roofed building, you can usually see the method of support for the covering. As stated above, a flexible material for the covering requires something like slabs of chip-board or tongue-and-groove boarding to guard against sagging.

Such supporting sheets often require support themselves, in the form of beams or girders of some kind, except in very small buildings. So you will find beams running across under the sheets.

The simplest beam is a length of timber, square or rectangular in section, and the behaviour of this kind of beam has been studied extensively. For a beam of rectangular cross-section, resting on supports at its ends, and carrying a load spread evenly along its length (a udl), the tendency to bend is zero at the ends and a maximum in the middle.

As mentioned earlier, the graph of the bending effect, plotted along the span, for this type of loading, follows a curve known as a parabola, one of the most beautiful curves in nature. This bending tends to squash the upper part and stretch the lower part of the section.

The middle part, i.e. along the centre line of the section, doesn't feel the bending stresses at all. This is why holes drilled through a beam for wiring or pipes for example, are made in the middle of the section. You may come across a beam with much of the web, (the plate joining the flanges) cut away, where the bending is taken care of by the flanges, and the shearing stresses are light. For the same reason, you might meet a beam built up from three sections to form a letter "I". Two plates form the flanges, the third piece being the web. Occasionally, too, the beams are of rectangular hollow sections.

The construction of a beam will depend to a large extent on the availability of different materials in the region.

In certain areas, for example, the use of bamboo cane has been brought to a fine art. Bamboo is a member of the family of grasses, perhaps one of the most important.

It is immensely strong and light for its size, and canes are available ranging from the tiny to the relatively enormous. A skilled worker in bamboo can produce anything from a parasol to scaffolding.

Because it is strong in both tension and compression, it is a versatile material, and is comparatively cheap, too. Its growth is vigorous, and it recovers rapidly from being cut down. Look out for examples of the use of this remarkable stuff, more especially in the warmer parts of the globe.

So a beam can be one solid piece, or built up from several parts. It can be of timber, plastic, iron, steel, aluminium, duralumin, or pretty well anything except jelly. It can be welded, riveted, glued, extruded, nailed, or pegged. What a variety.

This might be a suitable place in which to say something about the way materials behave. We shall not go into it very deeply, but it might help you to appreciate what is happening in a roof structure if you know something of what happens under stress.

Perhaps it will help if you get hold of a rubber band, and cut it so as to have a strip of rubber in your hand. If you hold one end, and pull on the other, gently and slowly increasing the pull, the strip will stretch. Let go, and it will return to its former shape. This is a demonstration of the property called *elasticity*. All materials possess this property to a greater or less extent.

We measure the elasticity of a material by the stress needed to produce unit strain. Put another way, if for a certain material, we plot a curve of stress against strain, the measure of elasticity is given by the slope of the straight part of the graph. For our rubber strip, the stress needed to double its length would be the elasticity for the rubber. Doubling the length is not difficult; but for some structural materials this is a theoretical figure, as breakage would occur at a much lower stress.

We recognise three types of stress: tensile, compressive and shear. These are not as independent as might appear at first sight. Perhaps we can show this by thinking of a steel rod, say, under tension.

The load on the ends produces a stress in the steel. A stress is measured by the force divided by the area. The bigger the force, and/or the smaller the area, the greater is the stress.

As the rod stretches, elastically, it shrinks laterally. The ratio of the two distortions, at right angles, is called the *Poisson's ratio*, after the famous scientist. Each material has its own value.

Inside, as the molecules are pulled apart in one direction, they are squeezed together in the direction at right angles. So tension along one axis is accompanied by compression at right angles. If you think of a little square piece, inside, there is a tensile stress on two opposite faces, with the compressive stress on the other two. If you now consider two adjacent faces, and their effect on a diagonal, you may see that there is a shear stress on the diagonal. So a simple pull can cause other stresses.

The point about the existence of these stresses is that some materials are weaker in tension, say, than in shear and vice versa. So something being pulled may fail in shear. A simple demonstration of this phenomenon is often used by lecturers who twist a stick of blackboard chalk, thus applying a shear stress across a diameter. Strong in shear, chalk is weak in tension. So you will see a tension failure along a helical line.

Again, if you get a chance to see a flat concrete roof or a beam, that has failed, you may see some of the reinforcement rods sloping up near the ends, indicating how the designer has had to take into account the directions of the resultant stresses.

Consider a section across a beam. The lowermost fibres are stressed in tension, and as we move up across the section, there is less and less stress till we reach zero at the middle. Continuing up, we find a compressive stress, which increases as we go further from the centre, reaching a maximum at the upper face.

You might feel from this that the top and bottom faces are the most important, and that the middle doesn't do much, so that we might as well cut out the middle. This is true, to some extent, and some large beams do indeed have some material removed from the middle.

They might even go as far as having almost no middle, just two separate members spaced apart vertically by braces, approaching a girder form, with which we shall deal later.

Looking again at the way the stress is spread across the section, and recalling that the bending effects are mostly in the middle of the span, and least towards the ends, it might seem reasonable to reduce the amount of material as we go further from the middle of the beam towards the end supports. So we could have a beam which tapers, narrowing towards its supports; and you may indeed see some like this. For the smaller beams, however, it is uneconomic to shape it, for the saving in cost of the material is offset by the labour charges involved.

Looking up at the inside of a small shed roof, then, you will probably see a few lengths of square sectioned timber supporting the boarding which carries the roofing material. Where this latter is rigid, it may be nailed directly onto the beams.

The spacing of these beams must be such that there is no sagging between them. In a small shed, this is judged by the eye of experience. For larger buildings, the spacing is calculated to minimise sag between the beams.

The simple beam is adequate for most small buildings like garden sheds, or the little inelegant but nonetheless attractive shelters on allotments, cobbled up from old bed-heads and whatever is to hand. For larger structures, you may see rolled steel sections used. These are usually I-sections, or L-sections, painted against corrosion, and bedded on plates at the walls.

Rolled steel sections are versatile and adaptable. A couple of L-sections placed back to back form a sturdy T-section, for example. The cunning choice and assembly of various sections can produce a very strong yet lightweight beam.

It would then require perhaps some small welding tacks or bolts to hold it all together. You may see this kind of thing in a roof which, while not strictly flat, rises only a little in the centre. One of the attractions of rolled sections is that their properties are listed, and some standard arrangements are listed, too.

For a wide flat roof we make use of girders, of timber or steel, so that there is some depth to the support. The idea is to separate the pushing forces on the upper side from the pulling forces on the lower side, to give them some leverage, to resist the bending. Perhaps the simplest of these is the Warren girder, that masterpiece of simplicity. You will bump into Warren girders all over the place.

Students of engineering and architecture swot away over examples of Warren girders; but an experienced man can assess the loading at a glance, if he recalls a little of the trigonometry thumped into him in his early school days. You see, all the triangles in a straight Warren girder are equilateral, so all the members are either horizontal or slope away at 60 degrees from the node, or junction, of the members.

An experienced engineer could look at a simple loaded Warren girder, and tell you the loading of each member pretty accurately without recourse to paper or a calculator.

It all looks impressively mysterious to the uninitiated, but here is how it is done, suitably simplified. (If you have an allergic reaction to mathematics, just jump a paragraph or two.)

Think of one end of a simple, symmetrically loaded Warren girder, the end node, with one member horizontal, and one sloping up at 60 degrees. There is a vertical supporting force there equal to half the weight of the roof.

Now draw, or just imagine, a triangle with the sides parallel with the members at that node. Since this is a right angled triangle with angles of 60 and 30 degrees, the sides are in the proportion of 1, 2 and $\sqrt{3}$ and the forces in the members are in the same ratio. If the vertical force is, say, $\sqrt{3}$, then the force in the horizontal member is 1, and in the sloping member 2.

So an experienced engineer could say that if the supporting force at the end were, say, 10 somethings, then the sloping member would carry a force of about 11.5 somethings, and the horizontal tie about 5.7 somethings. Wonderful stuff, some of this elementary trigonometry.

The way an engineer would work out these amounts would be like this: as the vertical force at the node is 10, then by proportion, the sloping member must carry 2 x 10/$\div$3. Multiplying this by $\sqrt{3}/\sqrt{3}$, we have 2x10x$\sqrt{3}$/3. Most engineers know that $\sqrt{3}$ is 1.732, so the quantity is simply 2x17.32/3 which comes to 34.32/3, say 11.4. It is really all very simple, once you know how.

You can work along the girder using this kind of argument for the other nodes, and so find the loading for all of the members. So when you look up inside a roof which is carried by Warren girders, you can tell what kind of load each member carries. There are several ways of deciding which members are ties (sustaining tension or stretching) and which are struts (taking compression or squeezing), but most experienced people working in the field can tell you which are which just by casting a knowing eye over the girder.

If you think of a particular member being cut away, causing collapse, you can usually see whether that member would have been pushing or pulling at the node, or junction. If the nodes need to be pushed apart, then the member would be a strut, and vice versa.

There are many other types of girder in use, and perhaps the next well-known type to consider is the Pratt, or N-type. Such girders consist of a series of rectangular panels, each braced by a diagonal member. A Pratt girder is simple enough, but the members are not all the same length, as they are in the Warren type. There are usually three different lengths in a parallel Pratt girder: the uprights, the horizontals, and the sloping members. If the panels of a girder are square, only two lengths are required.

When an engineer employs such a girder to support a flat roof, he may metaphorically "pull one out of the drawer". Firms which specialise in such structures build up a "library" of girder designs to cope with various loading demands.

When clients submit their requirements, they can often be met at once by a design that may require nothing more than a scaling up or down to suit the size and loading of the particular roof. In this way a specialist firm can submit a competitive tender quickly. A firm which must design from the beginning is at an obvious disadvantage.

Girders such as Warren and Pratt types may be of metal tubing, angle iron, or wood, and may be parallel, or diminished towards the ends. They may have curved outer members, and you may come across them in vertical structures. They are excellent structures, weight-saving and efficient.

Sometimes you may come across girders built like a lattice, the sloping members crossing one another, with no vertical members. These often display what are known as *redundancies*, i.e. more members than are really demanded by basic analysis. Look out for these at railway stations. Some of the old railway building was over-designed, to be on the side of safety, or for aesthetic reasons.

The roof loading is conveyed to the girder at the nodes, for the members are not designed to take lateral forces. The nodes can be constrained by *gusset plates*, small plates to which the ends of the members are riveted or welded. This leads to secondary loading. Sometimes the nodes are simple pin joints.

Besides the method outlined above, there are other ways of finding the loads in the members.

An easy way for the beginner to understand is one where we imagine a particular member cut through, so that the girder tends to collapse. Then we work out what force would be needed to prevent the collapse, and this is the force in the member considered. To understand this, we must get hold of the idea of "moments".

A force tends to move a piece of a structure in two ways, (i) forwards, and (ii) round a point. The tendency of a force to turn something round a point is called the *turning effect*, or the *turning moment*. The turning moment, or simply the *moment* of a force is the amount of force multiplied by its leverage.

In any assembly, all the moments round a point must add up to zero. We write this simply as "The sum of the moments about any chosen point is zero", or

$$\sum M = 0.$$

Then, looking at all the forces, and all their leverages, we can write down something like this:

$$(F1 \times d1) + (F2 \times d2) + (F3 \times d3) + \ldots = 0.$$

From this equation we can readily find the unknown force. We shall look at some examples of this later.

You can think of the strength of a girder, to cope with bending, as coming from the vertical space between the top and bottom members. The farther apart they are, within limits, the better is the girder able to resist the loading. A long span or heavy loading demands a deep beam or girder. As you look up inside a roof here and there, you will be able to appreciate this.

Beams can fail either (i) through the upper or lower parts being pulled or squeezed beyond their strength or (ii) the middle part shearing vertically, or (iii) the combined effect of bending and shear imposing a stress (compressive, tensile, or shear) somewhere in the material. The same thing applies to girders of any kind.

At any point in a piece of material, the stresses due to bending, shear, tension and compression combine to produce a complex system. This can be analysed to find what is going to cause concern.

Another way of dealing with a long span is to brace the beams or girders, running the bracing struts from part way along the span to the ground, or part way up the walls. Since this interferes with the free space beneath the roof, this is acceptable only in special cases. Look out for them. They are not plentiful.

As mentioned above, a draw-back of the flat roof is its inability to throw off rain. As a result, pools of water form, and these can lead to deterioration of the covering material. Once there is a hole in it, water can get through to the support beneath, leading to corrosion and failure. This is the reason for choosing an impermeable covering.

As mentioned previously, a commonly-used cladding is roofing felt. It is supplied in rolls, so must be laid in strips. The joins are vulnerable areas, and need careful sealing.

Once felt is damaged on a flat roof it is usually better to replace the whole sheet. The material is not everlasting and as it is very cheap, compared with other materials, periodical replacement can be a wise precaution, even though there is no obvious damage. This is called "preventive maintenance".

We have spent some time on the flat roof, though in practice you may not see many of them. We have dwelt on it at some length, as it brings up some of the principals applicable to other types of covering.

Before leaving this section we must draw attention to the use of lead as an impervious material for covering.

Although the word "plumber" is usually associated with domestic piping, it is derived from the Latin word for lead, and a plumber is one skilled in working with lead, wherever it might be used.

Lead is an unusual metal in that it is soft and malleable at ordinary temperatures, yet melts under comparatively low heat, and it welds readily. You are most likely to find it used on the flat, or almost flat, roof of a church tower.

In the past, when lead fetched a good price, this has provided an easy target for thieves. The resultant damage and leakage proved expensive for church authorises. Used as an impermeable sheet for protection, it is used for flashing, and sometimes for damp-proof courses.

Lead is a very heavy metal, and is usually laid over boarding. For smallish areas, stout boarding requires no further support, so you do not often find beams or girders below a small lead roof. The material is used for *flashing*, too, tucked into joints in brickwork, and for *drips*, to carry water over the edges of roofing. At the other extreme, perhaps the lightest roofing material is a modern plastic.

Corrugated for strength, it may be transparent to allow light below, though the transparent version does tend to discolouration after a time. Patches of yellow and brown appear, and make it look somewhat tatty.

It is possible to cover a flat roof with timber, planking it and serving the seams with caulking. You will finds this chiefly on boats, where the saloon or cabin is protected under the side decks with this kind of covering. A beautiful laid deck in good condition is a delightful and inspiring sight, though the word "roof" is not used afloat, save when referring to the coach roof over the cabin.

Large spaces on a flat roof can soon show puddles when it rains. These puddles can harbour nasties that can eat through almost any roofing material in time.

On occasions, an architect may design a low wall or *parapet* to run round the outside of a roof, so that from below it may seem that the roof is flat. Within the parapet there may be a flat roof, or one with ridges, or perhaps walkways. In some places, you can find a row of buildings with parapets.

Here, the general effect can be pleasing, an even roof-line running along the street. This is particularly noticeable when the buildings are of the same height. This is a town scene, and hardly ever seen in rural districts.

A flat roof may be used to accommodate oddments for which there is no room inside the building. So tanks, ventilation trunks, lift winding gear and so on may find suitable places there.

If they are set back from the edge, they are not normally visible; but if such excrescences are sited near the parapet, if any, they can be unsightly. Look out for them in towns.

Recall

1. What kind of stress does the upper flange of a beam carry?

2. Name two types of girder.

3. Why are some "flat" roof structures not quite flat?

4. How may a beam fail under load?

5. What do you understand by the term "bending moment"?

6. Comment on the suitability of corrugated iron sheets for roofing.

7. What is a parapet?

8. At one end of a Warren girder, the upward supporting force is 30 units. What are the forces in the two members meeting at that node?

9. Whereabouts in the web of a steel girder would you drill a hole for an electric cable or a pipe run?

10. Name some advantages of corrugated plastic sheets.

The Pitched Roof

When we turn from the flat roof, we can see the pitched, or sloping roof, with a tilted surface to ensure the shedding of rain and snow. Although the flat roof is satisfactory in dry climates, we need a slope in the less arid parts of the world, and that is where we shall find them. There is no shortage of this kind of structure. Vast housing estates all over the country provide numerous examples, often a dull succession of rows and rows of identical shapes, uniformly smothered in slate or tile.

The most interesting part of a roof is, of course, what you can see inside. Sometimes this is covered by what is known as the ceiling, a covering to hide the structural members. You have to get above the ceiling into the attic, to see what is holding up the roof itself. Here you may see roof supports, perhaps rafters, stout members upon which are fixed lighter strips called *purlins*. There may be slates or tiles attached to the purlins, or roofing felt; and you can perhaps find some trusses there.

In the attics of the average house there is usually a pile of discarded packaging that, optimistically, "will come in useful one day", and rarely does. There you can find travel gear, trunks, suitcases and the like, spare rolls of wallpaper for patching that might be needed if there is a tear, but fade away neglected, Christmas decorations, empty large boxes that once held computers; all find their way into the attic. They all add to fire risk, of course; but in a small house, the attic offers perhaps the only suitable space for this kind of storage.

You may find some attics converted into extra living accommodation, a study perhaps, or an extra bedroom. The beams can be covered with a light flooring for this, and sometimes a dormer window fitted. Here, too, between the beams, you may see thick insulating material, to help to insulate the house against outside extremes of temperature. This does lead to the attic being a very cold place, so the water cistern is usually covered carefully.

If the insulation is laid between the rafters, instead of between the beams, the attic is not so likely to become a refrigerated space; but it is more difficult to set the insulation in the sloping spaces, and more material is needed.

In choosing the degree of slope for a ridged roof, there are several factors to consider. The steeper the slope, the faster will the rain run down to the gutters; but the more covering material will be required. Again, lighter rafters can be used on a steep slope, though they will be longer. For a slated or tiled roof, there is a minimum slope which is effective. Anything less will invite water to make its way up between the slates or tiles, either by capillary action or blown by the wind. It is not only water dropping vertically that threatens the integrity of the covering.

Damage to the covering, such as a loose tile or slate, invites a steady stream through the roof, which is good for trade but expensive for the owner. Although roof timbers can be treated against rot, they do not thrive when subjected to water percolation. A slater can readily replace a broken slate, using a long flat tool that he slips up between slates, and with a hooked part at the end, with which he can cut fastening nails.

Generally the inclination of the roof is about 30 degrees, or about 1 in 1.7, but there are many variations. A very steep roof, though not contributing very much to the utility of the structure, can be striking and attractive, giving the building a distinctive character if set among buildings with shallower slopes. Further, it can provide extra space for living or storage.

A very shallow slope may demand stout girders or beams to support the load, and it can impose an outward thrust on the walls, requiring special attention to their design. On the other hand, a very steep roof, though picturesque, may prove expensive; and if the roof is narrow it may not be possible to make good use of the attic space.

Many roof designs are just "pulled out of the drawer", when a firm is occupied in the preparation of designs for more or less standard buildings. The firm has experience of what proves satisfactory, and just serves up "the same again". So roof trusses tend to be standardized, more or less, where dwellings are produced in quantity.

You may get a good idea of the optimum slope, or at least a satisfactory slope, from the timber trusses that you can see from time to time, being transported on lorries to building sites. They are factory made, stack neatly on a lorry, and are delivered to the various sites as required.

The simple ridge roof is like a pair of playing cards, leaning against one another, the kind of thing to be seen in a child's drawing book. When the cards collapse, the bottom edges slide outwards, and are indicative of the outward thrust at the bottom of a roof structure. In almost any community this kind of roof is to be seen in quantity. The covering is usually slate (real or imitation), tile, corrugated iron or asbestos, and is unremarkable, from the outside.

Looking along a row of buildings with this kind of roof, however, you can see many variations. Some will be pierced by dormers, some may have exaggerated slopes, for effect; some may have large overhanging eaves. Others may have the roof line set back at the lower end, with a parapet, and possibly a walkway. Again, there may be chimneys, fancy barge boards, and so on. Such items add to the variety and interest.

It doesn't cost a great deal more to fit decorative barge boards, and many people consider the increase in cost worth it, for the interesting appearance of the building. Modern methods of machining timber can turn out a barge board with an intriguing pattern of floral or other design, at not much more than the cost of a plain board.

The roof may intersect with the roof of additional rooms or extensions, so that valleys are introduced, adding some interest to a building that might otherwise seem rather plain. The valleys of such intersections demand special treatment, with provision of waterproof linings to carry away the rain.

The ridge, too, needs special treatment. You may sometime see older buildings where the ridge is no longer straight, and the ridging tiles follow a somewhat snake-like line. This indicates failure of the supporting structure; but a roof in this condition may continue to provide useful service for a long time.

In older buildings it is not unusual to see ridges than are more curvaceous that the original design. Sometimes they can stay like that for years. They are referred to as "quaint" by house agents.

In a small building, running along the centre, under the ridge there is a board on edge, that is with its long side vertical, connecting the rafters. This gives the board its greatest resistance to distortion by bending.

If you climb up into the loft, or stand in a small shed, looking up, you can see this. This is a happy place for spiders, though what they live on is a mystery, for there are few flies there. Perhaps they just eat one another.

From the outside, a ridged roof has some interesting features, especially if there be more than one ridge. The valleys are lined with some zinc, lead, or other impervious material, to carry away the water, and the hips are tiled to seal the roof there. At the end of the ridge you may find a decorative ridge tile, perhaps with a curly floral design, to mark its importance. This gives it a somewhat debonair appearance.

When you look under a roof you will see the means of support, the rafters, the trusses. Generally, there are three types of timber truss that you should bear in mind: king post, queen post and hammer beam.

The *king post* arrangement depends upon a vertical post at the middle of the truss. This strut connects the ridge to the centre of the tension member running across the span. They are often standardised, and made in quantity at a factory. The modern tendency is to assemble them with special metal fasteners, to save on labour. Timber flows in at one end of the factory, and a stream of trusses emerges at the other end, in a more or less continuous process.

The *queen post* provides more space in the middle. Instead of one vertical strut, there are two, leaving a space between them. This type of truss is less common, and is more likely to be seen in a roof with a longer span and in some older buildings.

The third type of truss mentioned above, the *hammer beam*, is a little more complicated. It is an expensive construction, with great curved members, and is to be seen in churches, and guild halls. You should enjoy looking at these, when you come across them.

Looking up at roof supports may give you a crick in the neck, so you may find it advantageous to stand at one end of the building, to get a more oblique view. The line of trusses marching along above the walls is impressive. In some of the older buildings they have been there for centuries, and the ancient builders are deserving of our respect.

They had tools that seem rather crude by today's standards, and lacked the power drills and electric saws that we enjoy nowadays. They were working in hard woods, too, not the soft deal used so much now.

The use of old ships' timbers for some cottages in seaside villages involved heavy beams and struts, often much stronger than the loading demanded by the layout. So you may see great lintels, and rafters, often with bits chiselled out to take other members. Such material was used for walls, too, the spaces between the timbering being filled with plaster of some kind. This can be seen in many English villages and lends an air of charm to a rural scene.

Thatch is a relatively light material, and the roof truss under thatch is not usually as stout as that carrying slate or tile. If you can get under a thatch, you will see that sometimes the support is altogether lighter. Thatch is thick, much thicker than the equivalent slate or tiled roof, but even so doesn't bear down on the supports so much.

Whatever kind of truss be used, there is a tendency to spread, pushing out the walls. The tension members in a structure are designed to resist this. In the case of a thatched roof, the walls are usually so thick that they take care of this easily. In other cases, it may sometimes be necessary to help by providing buttresses, to lean against the outside of the walls. You may see these in even small thatched cottages. A cob wall may have buttresses incorporated at the time of building.

Cob walls were common in earlier times, especially in villages. Reputedly, cow dung and mud were popular materials for making cob, but clay and chopped straw were used to build walls which were and are surprisingly endurable, if properly protected.

A cob wall is thick, and the wall plates that carry the roof rest on them, with the thatch carried out well clear, for cob walls must be kept dry. You may find a band of pitch around the bottom of the wall to help this. Although the outside of a cob wall is not usually as smooth as an ordinary plastered wall, and rarely extends upwards very far, it is an efficient means of supporting a roof. The occupants are cosy in winter and cool in summer.

Cob is not used with thatch only, and you may come across cob supporting other kinds of roof, sometimes replacements for thatch. Because of the thickness of a cob wall, it can withstand the outward thrust of a pitched roof, and can accommodate flues from chimneys which carry the smoke from fires, bread-ovens and ranges.

When we consider the loading of a truss, it may be helpful to think of the simplest of all, a plane triangle, the two sloping members taking the load of the roof, and the cross member dealing with the tension.

The loading can be considered as a uniformly distributed load (udl), bearing down on the rafters. So the rafters have to handle the bending and shearing affects of this load, and transmit them to the walls.

This loading means that the rafters are at the same time trying to spread, so they are tied by the horizontal member, which is in tension. If the load on each wall is half the weight of that section of the roof, then there is an upward thrust of that amount at the joint or node. If you draw a little triangle with sides parallel to this upwards thrust and the two members meeting there, you will have a scale drawing of the forces. The upright line represents to scale the thrust up from the wall; then the sloping line gives you, to the same scale, the force in the rafter, and the horizontal line the pull in the horizontal member.

I hope you will agree that this is all very simple. An experienced engineer or architect could do this kind of thing in his head. Because of the general standardisation of this kind of truss though, this is rarely necessary.

The next step in complication is to fit members which run from the bottom of the strut to the mid-points of the rafters, providing them with resistance to bending. This is a popular frame used in small houses, quickly and cheaply made, and effective. You will probably see more of these than any other type. You can buy these pretty well "off the shelf" from builders' merchants.

Large housing estates use them by the hundred. Nowadays they are usually treated against attacks by pests, and will last for years.

With increasing loads, the truss takes on more and/or stronger members, in general forming extra triangles. Triangulation is the basis of rigid structures, with a few exceptions. If four members are joined at their ends, forming a rectangle, it will not be rigid unless there is some fixing at the nodes, or corners, by nails or screws or the use of a gusset plate.

On the outside of a ridged roof, you will see laid out along the ridge the half-round, or shaped tiles that keep the ridge dry, and shed the rainwater down onto the roofing material.

Chimney stacks, usually of brick, that poke up through the sloping roof, require treatment to ensure that they are not the source of leakage. So lead flashing is used around the base of the brickwork; and you can see this clearly on low buildings. On the roof, therefore, you may have slaters fixing the slates, bricklayers building the stack, and plumbers dealing with the lead work. On a small building, or in a small firm, one man may fulfil all of these roles.

Dormer windows, too, have valleys that have to be lined to carry away the water. The lining is zinc, plastic or lead. Valleys occur, too, where a roof "turns a corner". Here again the valley has to be carefully constructed as a gutter or channel to carry the rainwater. The edges of the slates or tiles overhang these valleys.

Earlier, reference was made to the ability of experienced engineers to calculate rapidly the forces in the members of trusses.

It may be appropriate here to tell you something of the cunning ways used by trained and experienced engineers. They can often mystify the layman.

It is always useful to remember that the sides of a 45 right-angled triangle are in the ratio of 1, 1, $\sqrt{2}$, and those of 30 and 60 degrees, are proportional to 1, 2, $\sqrt{3}$.

Thus, for example, if you have a force triangle with angles of 30 and 60 degrees, then you know that the sloping force is twice that of the horizontal force. Further, the vertical force is $\sqrt{3}$ times the horizontal force; and the value of $\sqrt{3}$ is 1.732, as every engineer knows. So if the horizontal force were, say 100, then the force in the sloping member would be 173.2, say 175 approximately.

The same sort of reasoning can be applied to cases where there is a 45 degree triangle. The sloping part is always $\sqrt{2}$ times the other two sides of this kind of triangle, i.e., about 1.4 times. For rough estimates this is a little under one and a half times.

For example, the diagonal of a square room is nearly one and a half times the length of one side. You don't really need a calculator for this! Similarly, if the roof slope is 45 degrees, say, then the sloping part is 1.4 times the height to the ridge.

However, the cunning and experienced engineer has other tricks up his sleeve. For quick and fairly accurate calculations, there are the obvious ones like multiplying by, say, 99, where we take a hundred times and take off a hundredth. For instance, 99 times 55? Simple. 5500-55, or 5445. A good engineer can stand beside a building or a drawing of one, and produce all kinds of useful information at the drop of a hat, with his hands in his pockets, while smoking a pipe, or even blowing the froth off the top of a pint.

There are those useful approximations like 9, or 10, for the gravitational constant, g, when using the metric system. In the Imperial system of measurement 33, or even 30, isn't a bad approximation.

Again, the value of π^2 is not far off 10, and that is good enough for many calculations. For small angles θ, the value of $\sin \theta$ is pretty close to θ itself, if the angle is in radians. This is all good useful stuff.

Suppose you want the square root of a number, and you are prepared to sacrifice a little accuracy. There are methods that may astonish the uninitiated. Take, for example, the square root of 50. This is the same as the square root of the quantity [7 x (50/7)], say [7 x 7.14]. If you take the average of 7 and 7.14, which is 7.07, you won't be far out.

Look up the square root of 50 in some tables, to see what I mean. It takes a long time to explain, but it works like a flash.

Take another example, say, the square root of your age. Make a near guess, as we did above, and divide this into your age. Take the mean, and that won't be far from the actual square root. Just try a few other numbers and see for yourself. Pocket calculators can sometimes seem redundant.

If you have a roof of span, say, 10 metres, and a rise of 2 metres, then from Pythagoras, the length of rafter will be given by the square root of 25 (half span squared) + 4 (rise squared), i.e. the square root of 29. Make a guess, of 5, say; then the answer will be about halfway between 5 and 29/5, i.e. between 5 and 5.8, say 5.6 metres. This is not very far out (about 4%) from the true value, 5.385, good enough for many purposes.

In the old days, one might use a slide rule, and nowadays a pocket calculator; but the ability to calculate things like this rapidly and accurately in your head is useful. Looking at a roof, you may soon be able to work out quite a lot of information mentally, and surprise your partner.

If you are familiar with algebra, you can use some of those relationships like $(a + b)^2 = a^2 + 2ab + b^2$ occasionally. If the b part is small, then the square of b is negligible, and can often be thrown away.

For example, to find the cross-sectional area of a beam 4.2 x 4.2, you can write it as the square of (4 + 0.2), i.e. 16 + 2 x 4 x 0.2, very nearly, or just 16+1.6, which is 17.6. This isn't very different from the true amount, 17.64; good enough for a rough mental calculation.

We don't want to labour the point but I do hope you can see that it is possible to scan a structure, or a proposed structure, and work out much of the necessary sizes and stresses without waving a calculator around the place.

You can see, I trust, from what has been written above, the value of a little background mathematical knowledge. There is a multitude of other tricky ideas to help. In the days before the pocket calculator, you could use your slide rule for scratching your head as often as for making calculations.

The pitched roof is very amenable to variations in design for aesthetic or other reasons. Round, square, or oblong in plan, once you have decided what you want for a roof, you can make changes easily to the size or appearance. Inside, the supporting structure is usually interesting to the roof watcher because of the variety of means used to hold up the covering. The choice of truss is determined to a certain extent by the space beneath, and by whether or not a ceiling is to be fitted.

When you look under a roof, you may well decide what motivated the designer in planning the support. For example, industrial buildings must often make provision for gantries and other equipment, agricultural buildings might need special ventilation systems, and so on. All this applies not only to ridge roofing, of course, but also to any type of roof.

Roof watchers are especially alert when there is construction work going on, for it is then that the supporting members are most easily seen. Building sites are dangerous places, though, and if a site is a "hard hat area", it is better to keep clear.

Recall

1. Where would you find a king post?

2. What do we mean by "flashing", and where can you see it?

3. Where can you see hips and valleys, and what is the difference?

4. Name three kinds of truss.

5. Work out, mentally, the approximate value of the square of 9.9, and compare it with the true value.

6. The vertical load at the end of a Warren girder is 200 kg. In your head, work out the forces in the two members at that node.

7. How would you recognise a cob wall?

8. Where would you look for a barge board?

9. What is a purlin?

The Vaulted Roof

The flat roof and the pitched roof can provide protection from the elements, and can be attractive; but they cannot approach the vaulted roof for beauty. Sometimes you can see a vaulted structure which for sheer magnificence has you agog.

The basis of a roof of this kind is the arch, a structural feature met in many forms. Perhaps the simplest way to approach this is to consider a horizontal load-bearing beam, supported at its ends by a pair of vertical forces. The beam exerts no horizontal forces on its supports, and all the forces are vertical.

Now suppose the beam to be bent upwards, into a curved shape, by pushing horizontally at the ends. When the load comes on to the arch, the outer ends of this curve will tend to spread, increasing the horizontal forces on the supports more and more as the load increases. You can imagine these inward forces at the ends, forcing up the arch. The actual shape of the arch is not necessarily part of a circle. It may be parabolic, or elliptical, or almost any other shape.

The building of arches seems to have been a matter of fashion, according to the people who were about at the time. The Romans built simple semi-circular arches, but the Goths had a point on theirs. The Gothic arch is to be seen in the windows of most English churches, and is unmistakable.

Another kind of arch that is easily recognised is the Moorish arch, where the intrados consists of a series of circular arcs. This is not found as a roof support, but in windows and doors. It is striking, and interesting, but costly to build. Often richly decorated, you come across it in the East. Occasionally the pattern strays westwards, where large numbers of immigrants like to bring their customs.

An arch need not conform to any of the classic forms, of course. The two extremes are the beam, and the simple ridge of two rafters. For sheer architectural beauty, as exemplified on large church buildings, the pointed arch is superb.

If a roof exerts a uniformly distributed load (udl) across the span, the graph of the bending effect is parabolic.

This means that when we draw a graph of the bending effect on a base of the span, the curve is a parabola, a common curve in nature, and perhaps the most lovely. If we build an arch to follow this curve, that is a parabolic arch, we have an arch where there is no bending effect anywhere. The loads on the parts of the arch are compressive everywhere.

A parabolic arch is not difficult to recognise. If you squirt the flow from a hose in an upward direction, away from you, the water will follow a parabolic curve. Look at it carefully; that is the shape of a parabolic arch. It may be flat or very high in the middle, depending upon the angle at which you point the hose, and upon the power of the jet, but the curve is smooth. If mathematics doesn't disturb you, you may like to know that the curve can be expressed as a simple quadratic, $y^2 = kx$. Take a suitable value for k, perhaps 1, for simplicity, and plot some corresponding values of x and y. Join up the dots and you will have drawn a parabola.

Although it is not often used for a roof, an arch may consist of three arcs, running into one another smoothly. You are more likely to see this in a railway bridge.

With the availability of special sections, a suitable steel girder can be used to support a roof of a very large span. This is particularly useful for covering an indoor arena, or sports hall, where the covering is comparatively light. The central rise can be so slight as to be not far removed from the shape of a flat roof.

If the roof loading were transferred to the supports at a single point, in the middle, then the simplest way to achieve compressive forces throughout would be to use a triangular frame. For any other kind of loading, we could avoid bending effects by shaping the roof support suitably. So we might use an elliptic arch form, or a curve having several arcs. Indeed, we might make up our arch from a number of straight lengths, all struts, to deal with a number of point loads. So you might find an arch with no curves!

Apart from roofing, you may find interest in the arches underneath bridges. These will give you some ideas of the variety possible. You can see some lovely cast iron arches in some of the Victorian industrial buildings. These arches often support longitudinal members which themselves provide support for rows of arches taking the roof load.

Old railway stations are fruitful sources of vaulted roofing. This is because the high vaulted structure provided better space for the dispersal of the smoke from those old coal-fired locomotives. Prowling around some of the large stations may provide much food for thought for the roof watcher. Often, the roofing material consisted of glass plates, to provide light to the otherwise gloomy space below.

Although the old Crystal Palace in London was destroyed long ago, some pictures exist of this remarkable structure. Here is a glass roof worth examination. See how the roof was constructed, and how it was supported. Our Victorian forefathers certainly knew a thing or two.

In the case of a beam, there is a tendency to bend, and to shear. The forces in a suitable arch, on the other hand, can be arranged to be compressive, running through the arch, so that there is no tension anywhere. Thus, the material can be something that can cope with compression, but not tension. A course of bricks, with mortar between each, is admirable for this. A complete row of bricks or stones can be set up, and take compressive loads. So we could build arches of brick or stone, or concrete even, without any reinforcement, and often do.

Let us think about a simple brick arch. In order to construct such an arch we must first set up a shape, called *formwork* or *shuttering,* or *centring,* of wood or some other suitable material, on which to lay our bricks while we are doing the actual building. This shuttering is of the desired arch form, and is strong enough to support all the bricks and mortar which are to be placed on it.

As the brick arch nears completion, the load on the shuttering increases, and the bricks are forced upon one another. The last brick, which closes the arch, is called the *keystone,* and it is not until this brick is fitted that the shuttering can be removed safely. Sometimes this keystone is a special tapered or decorated brick. Although plain bricks can be used to build an arch, the joints are then tapered; but tapered bricks or *voussoirs,* may be used, so that the mortar at the joints is even. The purpose of the mortar is to transfer the load between the bricks or stones, accommodating the irregularities of their surfaces. Arches like this, of brick or stone, may support a roof, over a colonnade.

All arches exert an end thrust, a horizontal force, on their supports. The smaller the rise, the larger is the end thrust. Long spans and low rise arches need special attention.

One way to appreciate this is to imagine an arch in the act of collapsing. As it falls, it spreads the ends apart, since the length of the arch is greater than the span; so there must be some horizontal inwards force to oppose this. Thick walls are capable of taking quite a big thrust at the ends, but often special supports, or buttresses are used. In some buildings, this thrust can be taken by ties, beneath the floor, providing an elegant solution to the problem. In effect, the tie is like the string of a bow, and this kind of set-up is referred to as a *bow-string arch.* The ends of the arch rib are below the ground surface, and the tie can be completely hidden.

The arch is useful where a clear span is required beneath the roof. A fairly flat arch demands a deep girder, of course, but this need not be unsightly. A large area such as an indoor bowling green, requires a clear space, free from supporting columns, and a fairly flat arch permits a low roof to be used. There are some good examples to be seen, though not among domestic buildings.

A vaulted roof can be a lovely thing. You can sit and admire it, lofty and often ethereal in appearance. The height lends an airy quality to the space beneath, and you will find vaulted roofing in churches and public buildings.

Support for a vaulted roof can be provided by hammer beams, which in effect form a kind of series of arches. These are usually beautiful, and in some of the old buildings where they are to be found are usually lovingly tended against the depredations of insects which eat wood wherever they can find it. Where you find hammer beams, linger and enjoy them. They are costly to build, but satisfying to the eye.

In some of the great cathedrals, high vaulted ceilings are built in stone. Sometimes you will find the stone arches running into one another like a curled fan, and these are delightful. They may be decorated with floral or angelic emblems, visible only with field glasses. You may even see some mason's joke, a caricature of one of his workmates, and sometimes there are wonderfully painted bosses at the junctions of the arches.

When some of the old cathedrals were being constructed, modern scaffolding was not available. Long tree-trunk poles were used, lashed together with ropes. Working with aplomb at those great heights, on somewhat flimsy-looking networks of poles and rope, calls for our admiration.

Modern scaffolding is controlled by strict legislation. Planking must be properly placed, with boards set to prevent accidentally stepping off the sides, and all access must be as safe as regulations can make it.

The roofing supported by these vaulted structures is usually of slate; and lead is freely used to deal with rainwater. This led to gargoyles of strange and fearsome features. The weight of such roofing material is impressive, and the old masons had to employ massive arches and pillars to handle it. The past history of great buildings is not without failures, in both design and construction, and you may find accounts of these in the literature; but some of these magnificent buildings have survived many centuries.

Access to the roof of a cathedral can be gained through a series of steps and ladders. It is worth while seeking permission to climb up there, and see what the masons wrought. Pay special attention to the manner of dealing with the rainwater.

The vaulted roof may be crowned with ridged or conical covering. At such heights, it is subject to stresses arising from wind, sun and water. The wind loads tend to bend the whole structure, the sun may produce severe uneven heating, and the rain can attack the materials used. It is not the water itself that is the danger, but what the water may contain. Pollutants in the atmosphere may result in a weak acid being precipitated. Heavy hailstorms may produce stones large enough to do considerable damage to slates and guttering. Upkeep of these large buildings can be expensive.

The glass in dormer windows can be protected against hail by fine metal mesh, and generous guttering can deal with heavy rain-fall. Watch for these signs of care and protection when looking at a roof.

Perhaps the greatest achievement in the world of architecture is the dome. Here we have, effectively, a series of arches arranged in a circle. It is a lovely self-supporting structure, and in its simplest form consists of successive rings of masonry or brick, of decreasing diameter with height, following a curve so that the whole edifice is like half a ball. However, domes are rarely found in their "simplest" form. They may be richly decorated, surmounted by a cross or other feature, pierced by windows, with galleries inside.

When we build an arch, it is not self-sustaining until the last stone, the keystone, is in place. Such is not necessarily the case with a dome, though. Some domes can be erected without shuttering. An igloo, once used by the Eskimos, is a good example of this.

Igloos are among the most remarkable buildings to be made from local materials. Blocks of ice are laid out in a circle. Another circular layer of ice blocks of smaller diameter, is laid upon these, and the process continues until the familiar half-sphere shape is complete. Ice is a material that is plentiful and to hand, easily shaped, and ready to bond with adjacent blocks. The igloo provides shelter from wind, and soon warms up inside when a few people are present. It costs nothing but labour to build, is attractive and altogether worthy of admiration.

However, the igloo is fast disappearing. The old traditional way of life of the Inuit people has changed with increasing speed during the past century. Mechanised transport, and diminishing dependence upon reindeer, seal and fish have tilted the balance. Where timber was once a rare commodity, it can now be flown in easily and reliably; and other materials are now available which once were not to be found in the icy regions.

Well, we cannot build igloos everywhere. Plenty of ice is required, and sub-zero temperatures, available only in the restricted regions of the higher latitudes. So the dome, typical of colder areas, is not seen elsewhere except when built of wood, steel or stone. In the warmer regions, then, we find the dome surmounting important community buildings, churches, palaces, assembly rooms.

The outsides of domes are often striking, some of them being gilded, and intricately decorated; but inside they can be fascinating.

For the roof-watcher, access to the inside of domes is often easy, for they are rarely ceiled. Examine the manner in which the builders have arranged to support the considerable load of the dome itself You may need a pair of binoculars and a comfortable seat, to get the best view. Consider the great weight of the dome, and how it is supported. You may find a circle of columns taking the load.

Some domes carry at the top, on the outside, a sort of twiddly bit, an extra embellishment like a little look-out or arbour. There may be a figure in it, even. Ecclesiastical domes are usually surmounted by a large cross or a crescent.

Although the dome is not often a feature of a private house, it can be used with considerable effect to provide light to a large room or hall, and to add to the appearance of the building. Look for such domes in the larger type of country house.

You will probably find the support is in brick. Remember that a dome or an arch exerts a spreading force at its base. Look for the way this is accommodated. You will have no difficulty in getting views and details of the more famous domes, such as that of St. Paul's in London, or the Capitol in the USA. In the Middle and Far East, too, there are many very famous domes. Among the latter are some of the traditional "onion" shape, where the maximum diameter is above the base. Those that are gilded shine in the intense sunlight and are visible for miles.

Old timbers take on a dark attractive hue; but in some buildings this is thought to deprive the interior of light. In some churches, therefore, the inside of the vaulted roof has been ceiled. Where this is done, the arch is segmented, so that flat sheets of material can be fitted into place, concealing the timber structure of the roof. This is a pity, but if the sheeting is painted or colour-washed with a light colour, the feeling of light is enhanced. There has been a tendency in some church groups to lighten the interior of the buildings, and this has been one way of achieving this.

In great cathedral buildings, where the roof itself is supported on soaring columns, windows high up in the walls provide light during the day. At night, the old candelabra are insufficient for today's congregations, and powerful electric lighting systems have been installed. However, in some buildings, the old candles are still used in the choir stalls. They are inefficient, labour intensive, and costly in candles; but they have a great charm. The annual carol service at places like King's College Chapel in Cambridge, is an experience not to be missed.

The dome has always been a feature of important ecclesiastic buildings. It is impressive from inside as well as outside the structure. Even in these days of skyscraper building, a dome can stand out on the skyline.

The famous Millennium Dome which was constructed in London to house an exhibition was unusual in many ways.

It was of comparative modest rise, and the external supports sprouted upwards from the outer surface. Although it showed no signs of structural failure, it failed commercially, and suffered an unhappy and undignified life. There are plenty of pictures in the files taken during its construction, and these are worth some study. It was a novel undertaking and an innovative kind of dome.

If you lay a sheet of paper across a pair of supports, say a couple of books, it will sag in the middle, under its own weight. If, now, the paper is given a slight bow, so that it rises in the middle, not only will it not sag, but will even be able to sustain a small load. This is effectively what is known as a shell construction.

You may find a shell roof looking like a half-cylinder, or perhaps as a dome. A typical construction is a comparatively thin sheet of reinforced concrete, but sometimes you may see a plastic sheet used, or plastic panels fitted into a geometric pattern of short members. The latter is not, strictly speaking, a shell roof. A wonderful example of this is the Eden Project, in Cornwall. Here the designers have set out a number of domes like giant footballs, providing a translucent covered area in which to grow non-native plants of many kinds. It is well worth a visit.

The stress analysis for a shell roof depends upon the solution of a number of equations for little pieces of the shell. It is assumed that each piece can cope with tension or compression only, so that there is no bending of the pieces themselves beyond the shape as constructed. When complete, the shell is one continuous sheet, running across the enclosed space, with no supports beneath. The space covered is thus free from obstruction.

We should not forget to make reference to the type of flexible "roof" to be found in tents and some life rafts. Some of these depend upon guys and poles, and some are simply inflated. Poles are compression members, and guys are tension members of the structure. A guy cannot take compression, and triangulates the arrangement with the pole and the ground or base.

This type of roof is usually a ridge, but some are vaulted, using an inflated arch to support the water-proof membrane, or cloth. There have been some remarkable advances in the design and construction of a suitable roof for portable shelters like this. A browse through the catalogues of firms selling camping equipment and life rafts for small craft will indicate the scope of new ideas.

Perhaps the simplest form of arched roof is to be found where pigs are kept. The farmer supplies the swine with small shelters formed from arcs of corrugated iron. These are cheap and sturdy, and much appreciated by the animals. They are lightweight, readily stowed, and cheap to make. They are weather-proof, and give adequate shelter.

During the 1939 45 war many lives were saved by a similar construction having the ends in the ground, and covered with soil. These were the Anderson shelters, issued to householders in vulnerable areas, for erection in the garden. Each one provided a roof for a family in cramped but safe conditions. Of simple construction, they were cheap and easy to make, and were produced in thousands. The Anderson shelter was effectively a vaulted roof of the simplest kind, and immensely strong. Many of them survived the explosion of near misses, and preserved the lives of the occupants.

Another type of roof produced at the time was the Morrison shelter, a flat sheet of steel supported on steel legs. This properly belongs under the heading of flat roofing, and is mentioned here only because it is in one sense in the same category as the Anderson shelter.

Before leaving the subject of vaulted roofing, perhaps we should mention the beautiful tracery to be found in some of those lovely cathedrals with high vaulted work, decorated with great skill by the masons of former times. In some cases you can find the wonderful intricacies of stone arches rising and meeting one another in astonishing, moving enchantment.

You don't need to travel far to see these wonders, for they are well photographed. Many delightful books have been published by enthusiasts of photography and architecture. Other countries, too, have produced some astounding structures, and they in their turn have published some books of striking pictures.

Vaulted roofing has an attraction of its own; and here and there you may come across models of cathedrals and similar structures of surprising accuracy. Model makers have been fascinated by making intricate and faithful models of impressive buildings. Look out for them. They will widen your knowledge of the methods used to support coverings in various architectural achievements.

Recall

1. Name some ways in which the designer can accommodate end-thrust in an arch.

2. What is the purpose of mortar?

3. How would you recognise a Gothic arch?

4. What is a parabola?

5. What is meant by a "keystone"?

6. What factors might determine the choice of shape for an arch?

7. Differentiate between a dome and an arch construction.

8. If an arch is in danger of collapse, what steps might be taken to prevent it?

9. What is a Moorish arch?

10. Name some famous domes.

Supports

As we have seen in the previous sections, trusses, arches, or girders carry the roof generally; but these have themselves to be supported. For this purpose, we must erect columns, or build walls of some kind. A column, or pillar, is a vertical member, loaded axially, designed to carry a roof. A pilaster is effectively a short length of thickened wall, a kind of squarish projection in plan.

A roof is supported ultimately by the ground or foundation, of course. In some cases, a sloping roof may run right down to the ground, with no intermediate structure; and in warm climates, where the roof is made from large leaves, this is a very convenient way of dealing with the matter, though it does restrict the space inside.

A ridge tent works like this, too. The covering is stretched over the ridge pole, and pulled down to the ground. Then, the wise occupant will dig a little gully around the bottom, to collect the rain and lead it away. So the support for the roof in this case is the pole and ridge line. The bell tent, too, has usually a centre pole, and short "walls" that reach to the ground. Here, the canvas itself can be regarded as its own support, pulled out by guys.

If we use walls, they are topped by wall plates; and where pillars are used they are joined by beams or girders, to take the trusses. At one time, a popular approach was the use of "portal" frames, inverted U shaped structures, a row of these forming the supports for the roof, and you may still come across these, usually fabricated from steel sections.

Looking first at pillars, or columns, these may be of steel, brick or other suitable material, with plates fitted to the tops. The theory of columns has been well studied, and the behaviour of a column under load is well understood. Euler developed a theory which linked the buckling load with the cross-sectional shape and the material. The result of his work was a simple equation widely used by engineers and architects.

Whereas beams carry transverse loads, causing bending and shear stresses, columns cope with axial loads, applied at the ends. If we consider the extreme case of a very short column, it is a pad, and only compressive stresses are involved.

As we increase the length of the column, however, we reach a stage where the column starts to bow in the middle, or buckle, under load.

In the same way, if we take a slender strut, and apply a gradually increasing load, we shall meet a critical point where the strut fails by buckling. You can try this out for yourself. Take something like a long thin bamboo cane and, with one end on the ground, push down on the top, slowly increasing the load. Then, quite suddenly, you will see the cane buckle. Trying this with different lengths of cane you will soon see that the length is important.

Taking a bundle of such canes, tied or taped together, it is easy to see that a thicker strut can take a greater load. The cross-section of a column is important in resisting end thrust. It is not just the area itself, though, but the way in which the material is spread across the area. You may see this clearly if you place a sheet of paper on edge on a table. It cannot support a vertical load; but if you roll it into a tube, you have a strong column, though the cross-sectional area is the same.

If we use a tube, it will carry a greater load without buckling than a rod of the same cross-sectional area. A measure of the spread of the material is given by what is called the second moment of area, I, of the section, sometimes erroneously called the "moment of inertia". A hollow cylindrical column has a much greater value of I than a rod of the same cross-sectional area.

Consider a rod of diameter 6, say, and compare its critical load with a tube of the same cross-sectional area, but with material spread out as a tube of diameter 10, and thickness 1. Then the critical load for the tube will be about four and a half times that for the rod.

If a column consists of rolled sections, they are assembled to give the largest value of I when they are welded together.

Stone columns are nearly always solid, and classic columns vary not only in their proportions, but also in the decorations at the top. The plainest columns are the Tuscan, relatively short and squat, and the Doric ones are not very different. Ionic ones have curly bits at the top, and the Corinthian columns are richly decorated. The latter are slender, too, which entails the use of more of them in a building.

Look up these orders in any good book on architecture, or an encyclopaedia, to see how they differ from one another.

Notice how building in steel is a very different matter from raising structures in stone. Stone is strong in compression, and relatively weak in tension, especially at the joints. Roof supports made in stone, even today, generally follow the rules of the classical styles. You may find it interesting to look at some of the classic buildings, even more so the ancient ruins, to see how the old craftsmen coped with the problems of holding up a roof.

So we decide how much load our column must carry, and how high it must be, and then choose a value of I that suits the case being considered. If we make our pillars of steel sections, we can choose a section with a large I value. Books of standard sections can be consulted . The forced introduction of metric units rendered obsolete many of the British books of sections. You may come across them in jumble sales, and so on, and will find them instructive. Many a fine building has been erected, based on these. If you can get hold of a modern book of sections, so much the better; but for our purposes the age of the book doesn't matter much.

We find the load that each column is to carry by considering the roof loading, and the distance apart of the columns. Close-set pillars might each carry one end of a truss or girder mounted on a plate; if they are set farther apart, then they may be connected by a member running along their tops, on which the trusses may rest.

Columns transmit their load to the ground or foundation by pedestals, or plates, spreading the force so that the stress suits the ground. Some of the best places to see this are in those old railway stations, where huge cast iron columns, supporting the lofty roof, swell out near their bases, and are fancifully decorated in the Victorian fashion. (Cast iron was a popular material in Victorian times. It was used for all kinds of things, from cauldrons to bridges.) Look at the columns, and look at the roof. Both are rewarding.

Another way to support a roof is by the use of walls, of brick or stone. These may be arranged to incorporate columns. Brickwork offers many opportunities for embellishment, and a brick wall of good standard is a pleasure to see. The brick was a splendid ancient invention, and they have been used by the million. You can find out more about this in *Brick Watching* in the Watching series.

If a brick wall is used to sustain a roof, and not merely to fill in the spaces between pillars, i.e. if it is to be useful as well as decorative, it must be sufficiently substantial to do its job. So you may find a brick wall that is more than one brick thick. Sometimes, too, decoration demands the use of other than common bricks. Look for patterns, and decorative openings, and the special bricks used to achieve the various effects.

When we build a brick wall, we usually start a new course or layer at the ends, and work towards the middle, where we build in *closers* to fill the gaps that are less than the length of a brick. Normally these are not noticeable; but if you look carefully, you will be able to spot the closers, usually near the middle of each course.

Stone walls are rarely seen in modern buildings; but you will find them in older structures, especially churches. They are lovely. The old craftsmen laid their stones with care, whether using the softer materials like sandstone, or flint (often found in chalk regions), and other hard stone such as granite.

Stone walls use either dressed or rough ashlars. For the latter, a generous use of mortar is essential, to cushion the sharp protuberances of one stone against adjacent ones. Dressed stones demand the skills of a stone mason. His method of dressing a stone is, first, to prepare one face, the largest, making it flat and true. From this as a base, he will then square up an adjacent face, using mallet and chisel, smoothing the face square and true with the base.

His next step is to deal with a third face, square with the other two. Then he will prepare the remaining three faces parallel with the first three. The finished ashlar is a block, square or rectangular, carefully finished on all six faces. In the best quality work mortar is not really needed between the blocks. In some of the ancient examples of stone walls one can find it hard to insert a piece of paper between the blocks, they fit together so well.

Flint walls are attractive, and since they seem to last forever, there are plenty of old ones around. They are regional, plentiful in chalky areas, so that you won't see them in places where other materials are handy. Plenty of mortar is needed for a flint wall.

Many walls are not designed to carry loads, being just "fillers" between pillars of various kinds. You can easily distinguish these, for they are usually less robust.

True roof supporting walls are usually thicker, and often incorporate pillars or pilasters of the same or a different material.

Since we are dealing with Roof Watching, we shall not consider the walls in depth. There is more information in *Brick Watching* in this series.

Recall

1. What is meant by the "second moment of area"?

2. Where can you see a pilaster?

3. What purpose was served by an Anderson shelter?

4. Name two types of classical columns.

5. How would you recognise a Moorish arch?

6. What is a shell roof?

7. Where was the Millennium Dome erected?

8. For what was Euler famous?

9. What is a vaulted roof?

10. Where can you see the Eden Project?

Cladding

There is a wide choice of material for cladding a roof, though the choice is sometimes dictated by cost, availability of timber, slate, etc., or location. In what follows we shall, without delving too deeply, review the options.

The simplest roofing material is undoubtedly the large palm leaf. Providing good shelter against the heat of the sun, it is also remarkably efficient at shedding rain. It could hardly be cheaper, for it is free! Even the labour needed to put it in place is minimal, and a pleasure, to boot. Roofing with palm leaves is often a social affair. It appears to be part of the *dolce vita* with which we associate the sunnier areas of the globe.

Smaller structures roofed with leaves are simple buildings, quickly built, and not always regarded as permanent. The slope of the roof has to be steep enough to ensure the rapid disposal of the heavy rain that often occurs in tropical regions.

Even in temperate areas, though, a roof of leaves can be erected as a temporary shelter. The leaves being small, more of them are needed for good cover. Small leafy branches are laid with the thick ends uppermost, plentiful and steep. Campers can easily make a shelter like this (at the right time of the year, not after the leaves have fallen!)

Such leafy buildings often have walls, too, from similar materials, interwoven wattle, small branches, with possibly mud to help seal the gaps. The supports may be stout trunks, or saplings, if the covering is to stay for a while.

The wigwam or tepee is a conical shelter, with a flexible covering. It uses animal skins, supported on poles. This is a quickly erected and easily transported abode. At the top is a vent to carry away the smoke from the interior. The Red Indians of North America, with whom this special kind of roofing is associated, had no wheeled traffic. Instead, they used an ingenious device, a couple of long poles, trailed behind a horse, called a *travois*. This needed no road or even hard ground, and bumped along happily wherever the horse took it. This kind of transport suited the wigwam very well.

The tepee can be quickly rolled up and stowed on the travois. A Red Indian family could break camp and melt away with ease. What a compact way of life for the wanderer. All that has been trampled by the ways of modern life, and the Red Indian of today may well be found, with his family, in a smart permanent building. The tepee has become little more than an interesting tourist attraction, more often than not fake.

In the same way, the igloo is no longer the hallmark of the Arctic regions. Roofing of ice and of hides is no longer as accessible as it once was.

Mention was made earlier of the uses of reed in thatched covering. Although an ancient craft, thatching is still carried on, and appears to have a healthy future. There are plenty of thatched properties to be found, and they all need maintenance. It is a sound cladding material, but it has to be renewed at intervals.

Slate is perhaps more widely used than any other material, when it can be readily obtained. In Britain, Wales is the chief supplier of slate. The men who work in the quarries are skilled at using simple tools to split and size the laminae, or sheets, which form the slate tiles. The names used for the different sizes of slate are given in the glossary. Slates are obtainable in the sizes shown, though you are not likely to see all of these. The demands of standardisation for the thousands of small buildings being erected throughout the land have inevitably led to a reduction in the sizes available. Slate is quite impermeable.

A slated roof is an excellent protection against the elements; and a good slater can cover a roof with astonishing rapidity. Lengths of wood are laid across the rafters, and the slates are hung from these, starting at the eaves, and working upwards to the ridge. The gaps between adjacent slates are covered by rows higher up the slope, so that water cannot penetrate. A slated roof is subject to two types of failure. Firstly, if the slates are hung on nails that can corrode, the nails will fail in time, and the slate will slide down the roof. Secondly, if wind can get under the slate, it can lift it and perhaps cause it to come loose. This can happen on the leeward side of a pitched roof, too.

As the wind whips over the roof, it creates an area of low pressure on the downwind side sufficient to lift the slate. Under severe conditions of storm, a slate roof may be stripped, with horrifying consequences for the inmates of the property.

Stone slabs have been used for cladding, and these are relatively heavy, and not easily dislodged. You will find these on low buildings in certain areas, ancient dwellings of stout construction.

The chief competitors to slates are clay tiles. These overlap at the edges, and if you examine one carefully you will find a couple of nibs along one edge, the upper edge, which fit along the wooden strips that support the tiles. Another edge is half curled, to fit over the adjacent tile. Clay roofing tiles are supplied in pink or green as a rule, and they are popular for large estates. Quickly fitted, and easily cut, a roof can be covered rapidly with clay tiles.

Like slate, tiles are impermeable. Although they can be disturbed by wind, they are not quite as vulnerable as slate. Some people regard a tiled roof as very attractive. You will find them used on walls, too. In some areas, the tiled wall is a regional feature. Tiles for walls usually have a lower edge suitably shaped to carry rain down, away from the edges.

There has been a growing tendency to use artificial slates. These have been made from asbestos sheeting and similar material, cut to the sizes required and shaped where required to fit the ends and edges of the roof. Such "slates" are a factory product, and are much less labour-intensive than the natural product. It is not difficult to spot them, for they are much more precise in appearance than the quarried stuff. They are naturally much cheaper, and some people feel that this shows.

In small villages, there is usually plenty of variety in roofing material, but in towns and cities where large numbers of identical dwellings are required, one can see vast stretches of roofing of a uniform appearance, acres and acres of slate, with rows and rows of pink tiles covering the more opulent houses.

The keen roof watcher will come across this kind of scene frequently, broken here and there by the starkness of some commercial building.

Daring architects occasionally get their way, and some very odd-shaped buildings get past the planning committees with steeply sloped sheets of glass and concrete, mixing roof and walls in a bewildering array, out of harmony with the surroundings, according to some people.

A flat sheet of material can be given some rigidity by creasing, folding, or bowing. So you may find a roof over a small area using a bowed piece of flexible material. Carrying this principle further, corrugations can be introduced, providing stiffness in one direction. Such corrugated material finds favour for roofing, with the ridges running down the slope.

At one time, asbestos cement was popular for this. Then the health hazards of asbestos were realised. Asbestosis is a killer, and many workers with the material suffered grievously. Steps were taken to pull down and destroy the large amounts of asbestos cement then in use. You will not find much of it about nowadays.

Another candidate for corrugating is steel sheet. Oddly, it is often called "corrugated iron", or even "tin". The latter arises from the tinning process applied to steel as a rust preventative. This is widely used in fruit canning. The cans are made from tinned steel sheet, and for brevity are called "tins". So sheds using corrugated steel roofing are frequently called "tin sheds". Roofing sheets are galvanised, i.e. coated with zinc, but the term "tin" still persists.

The term "tin shed" is often used in a disparaging way; but roofing of corrugated steel is really very good. It is impervious to rainwater, easily fitted, and needs no maintenance. All corrugated sheeting is fixed by nails driven through the ridges, and never the valleys. The heads of the nails often carry small felt washers, so that rain has little chance of penetrating.

When newly fitted, the roof is shiny, and rarely treated. So it soon loses its shine, and takes on entrancing hues of red, brown and gold. An old corrugated iron roof is charming. If left too long, the corrosion eats its way through the sheets, to produce gaping holes. You will find this kind of thing on farms, in sheds and outhouses where a drop of rain doesn't matter very much anyway.

Disposal of worn corrugated iron roofing is simple. You just leave it to rust away completely. Ferrous compounds rapidly oxidise and return to the reddish ore.

Some plastics, too, are suitable for roofing. These are corrugated, with rectangular, trapezoidal, or semi-circular corrugations. Although normally white, they can be found in a variety of colours, with matching gutters and rainwater pipes.

From time to time new materials appear on the market, some of them very good. The old traditional slate and tile are in a strong position, though, and the producers continue to thrive. You will see more of this kind of roofing than any other.

You can get a good idea of what is happening in this field by glancing through the catalogues of builders' merchants. These catalogues are a veritable treasury of information, and make absorbing reading for the roof watcher. What is more, they are free!

Before leaving the subject of roof cladding, we must mention the use of glass and plastics to provide light and protection, in two special cases, both in England.

The Crystal Palace in London no longer exists, as it was destroyed by fire, but pictures of this amazing building may be seen. It was an excellent example of the skill, ingenuity, and assiduity of the Victorians. It was a large building, glazed throughout, so that the interior was light and airy, and was much enjoyed by the people of the day. The supporting structure was beautifully fashioned, and its loss was a sad event for the capital, and indeed for the country. It was, and perhaps still is, one of the best examples of a transparent roof to be seen.

The other example is also to be found in England, in the county of Cornwall. This is the Eden Project. Here we have a series of fully glazed buildings large enough to accommodate all kinds of exotic trees and plants. The intention was to provide a controlled environment to suit the various plants and insects which were to live there. Highly successful, it is well worth a visit, not only to examine this wonderful roofing, but also to enjoy the remarkable contents.

You are unlikely to see a roof of sods nowadays, but they have been used in the past. On Vancouver Island, in Canada, there is a commodious store with a roof covered with soil and grass, and a couple of goats to nibble it! It is a tourist attraction, but seems to be effective.

Recall

1. Discuss the reasons for choice of covering materials.

2. What is the purpose of corrugating a roofing material?

3. How might climate affect the selection of cladding?

4. What is a travois?

5. What is used to hold in place (a) slates, and (b) corrugated sheets?

6. In determining what slope to use on a roof, what factors might affect the decision?

7. What happens to the metal of a corrugated iron roof when it corrodes? What is the result?

8. What is the name of the smallest size of slate?

9. "A slate is a natural material, and a tile is the product of a process." Comment on this statement.

10. What are the merits and disadvantages of thatching?

Further Reading

There is plenty of material for the ardent roof watcher. Apart from all the books on building and architecture, there are references to roofing features in all the encyclopaediae, and in many other types of book as well.

Mention has already been made of trade catalogues. These can be a fruitful source of information. The firms are happy to give them to you. After all, you may want to buy some of their goods. It is also a good idea to number some builders among your friends. It is surprising what you may learn over a pint. In any case, a good roof watcher will soon find that his circle of knowledgeable friends widens more and more as he or she pursues this fascinating occupation.

Browse along the appropriate shelves in your local library. Occasionally, get a copy of *The Builder*, and other appropriate periodicals.

Major book sellers, like Amazon, issue lists from which you may find sources to help you.

Here are some suggestions for your reading on roofs:

Dobson, C. G. *The History of the Concrete Roofing Tile*. Batsford, London, 1959.

Millar, J. *Slating and Tiling*. (2nd edition) English Universities Press, London, 1947.

Molloy, E. *Roof Construction and Repair*. Newnes, London, 1941.

Wickersham, J. H. The David and Charles Manual of Roofing. David & Charles, Newton Abbot, 1987.

Here are some on thatching:

Billet, M. *Thatching and Thatched Buildings*. (2nd edition) Hale, London, 1988.

Nash, J. *Thatchers and Thatching*. Batsford, London, 1991.

West, R. C. *Thatch*. David & Charles, Newton Abbot, c. 1987.

Glossary

Beam A structural member designed to sustain transverse loads. Although in general a beam is horizontal, this is not essential. For example, a telegraph pole is in one sense a beam, since the wires and the wind act horizontally on the vertical pole. The pole is a cantilever beam, as well as being a strut, carrying the vertical loads.

Barge Boards Boards, often decorated, running from soffit to ridge, at the ends of the roof.

Batter The slope of a wall. This is particularly noticeable in retaining walls, for stability.

Bending Moment or **Bending Effect** The transverse forces on a beam cause it to bend, so that it is deformed. The effect at any point, due to a given force, is the amount of that force multiplied by its leverage about that point. Thus, a vertical force of 12 force units, operating at a distance of 10 length units from a certain point in the beam, would exert a bending effect, or moment, of 120 bending units. A rafter carries a uniformly distributed load, and the bending moment diagram is parabolic. Although the true meaning of "moment" is "effect" or "weight", as in "It is of no great moment", the word has been used on its own so often that the word "bending" is often omitted in structural circles.

Bitumen An inflammable mixture of hydrocarbons, such as naphtha, or petroleum. It is used to treat roofing felt.

Bressummer This is a great beam which supports most of the front of a building. In some rare cases it may form the horizontal member of a truss.

Brick A baked clay block, made to standard sizes, used to construct useful structures. A good bricklayer can produce very attractive work, quickly and efficiently. See *Brick Watching* in this series.

Buckling Load The load on a strut that causes it to bow, or buckle, the centre part moving outwards, and so becoming unstable.

Buttress To provide outside support, a wall may be reinforced by a distinct thickening at some points. If the buttress is clear of the wall except at the top, it is called a *flying buttress*.

Cantilever A beam with only one end fixed, like a diving board.

Column or Pillar A structural member designed to carry axial forces. It is usually vertical, and when it is at some other angle, it is called a *strut*.

Corbel A projection from a wall, like a very short shelf, to take a load from above, such as the end of a truss. Some corbels are decorated fancifully.

Corrugated Steel, plastic, and asbestos sheets can be supplied flat or corrugated, i.e. rippled in section to provide rigidity. Asbestos is not as popular as it once was, because of the associated risk of cancers. The corrugations are standard sections.

Dormer When the attic requires light, it is often provided by windows set into the sloping roof. These can be pretty additions to what might otherwise be a dull roof expanse. It is thought that the name was originally a "dormitory" window.

Eaves The projecting edge of a roof, just above the guttering. If no guttering is fitted, the eaves may overhang far enough to shed the rainwater well out from the walls.

Extrados The convex surface of an arch, as opposed to the *Intrados*, the concave surface.

Flying Buttress A buttress whose base is some distance out from the base of the wall, curving over to meet the wall nearer the roof.

Gable The end face of a ridge roof.

Gusset Plate A flat member, triangular or trapezoidal, used at a node to prevent relative movement. It may be of timber or steel, depending upon the material of the members.

Gutter A gutter is a channel for conveying water, and is found on a roof just below the eaves. The older gutters were of cast iron, though thatch was carried beyond the bottom of the slope far enough to ensure that the rain fell off clear of the wall. Modern guttering is usually of plastic, and may be of semicircular or square section. Guttering must have a fall towards one end, where the down-pipe is fitted.

Hammer Beam Roof This type of construction is unmistakable. It is expensive, but attractive, and is most often seen in churches. The curved members complete the triangulation required for stiffness.

Hip When the end of a roof slopes backward instead of ending in a gable, the external angle formed by the sides is called a hip.

Intrados The concave side of an arch.

King Post The vertical strut in a truss, connecting the ridge to the centre of the horizontal member. In small buildings, this is a commonly used type of truss.

Metope The frontal surface, often richly decorated, between the triglyphs (three-grooved tablets) of a Doric frieze. Seen only in classical or pseudo-classical buildings.

Moment See "Bending moment", above.

"N" Girder See "Pratt Girder".

Node The junction of a number of members in a structural frame.

Pilaster A pilaster looks like a column built into a wall. It thickens and strengthens the wall at that point.

Pillar See "Column" above.

Plane Frame A frame in which all members are in the same plane; a "flat" frame, as opposed to a space frame, e.g. a tripod. All triangles are plane frames. Adding members to a triangular arrangement may change it to a space frame if it is not kept flat.

Poisson's Ratio This is the ratio of the strains along mutually perpendicular axes. Thus, when a rod is compressed, the ratio of the diametrical strain to the longitudinal strain is the Poisson ratio for that material. The ratio is peculiar to each particular material.

Pratt Girder A girder in which the members form a series of "N"s, i.e. rectangular panels with diagonals. The proportions of the rectangles are arbitrary, and the members are proportioned according to the loads in them.

Purlin A light member running across the rafters, to which the roofing material, slate, tile, etc. is attached.

Queen Post In a queen post truss, there are two vertical struts, providing a clear space in the middle. The vertical members are often at quarter-span.

Rafter A beam running from the eaves to the ridge, designed to handle the roof loading. The purlins are laid across the rafters to provide supports for slates or tiles.

Roof Truss An assembly of members forming a structure, running across the span, on which roofing is supported. It is built up from members in steel or timber. Roof trusses are largely standardised, but are easily designed for special cases.

Shearing Force When a transverse load is applied to a beam or girder, it tends to shear or slice the member at that point. This tendency to shear varies in general along a beam. For a girder carrying a roof, the loading is generally nearly uniform, and the diagram for the shearing force is in the form of a double triangle. The shearing stress is the shearing force divided by the area on which it operates.

Shell Construction A thin layer, without external supports, usually as a part-cylinder or part-spherical shape, providing a clear space beneath.

Slate A material that is found in layers, skilfully split by workmen, to provide impervious slices for roofing and damp proof courses. Traditionally, they have been supplied in inch sizes as follows:

Doubles	13" x 6"
Ladies	16" x 8"
Viscountesses	18" x 10"
Countesses	20" x 10"
Marchionesses	2" x 12"
Duchesses	24" x 12"
Imperials	30" x 24"
Queens and Rags	36" x 28"

Soffit Although originally this meant a ceiling, it is now applied to the underside of an arch, entablature, bridge, or eaves.

Strain This is a measure of the deformation of a member, usually expressed as a ratio of the amount of deformation to the original dimension. Thus, a tie of length 1000 units, which stretches 1 unit, is said to have suffered a strain of 0.001. See "Stress" below.

Stress When a force is applied to a piece of material, the material is deformed, either elastically or plastically. The internal structure of the material is changed, and in trying to regain its former shape it undergoes resistant stress. Stress is measured in force on unit area. In lay terms, stress and strain are often synonymous, but technically they are quite different. See "Strain" above.

Strut A member in compression. If it is very short it becomes a pad. The length is governed by the tendency to instability, or bowing, when too long. The load-bearing capacity of a strut is dependent not only upon its cross-sectional area, but upon the shape of the cross-section, too. Thus, a strut of cylindrical section is stronger than a rod of the same cross-sectional area, since the material is set further from the axis. The instability of a long strut can be opposed by lateral support between the ends.

Thatch The use of straw or reed to produce a rain-resistant roof. Not so common nowadays, due to the cost of labour, this method of roofing was at one time widely used in areas where other types of roofing material were not available. It is a fire risk, but otherwise has advantages in appearance, and water-shedding. Its insulating qualities are diminished by the flow of air through it.

Tie A member which is undergoing stretch when loaded. The shape of the cross-section is relatively unimportant, and ties are often designed from rod or bar. Timber ties need careful attention at the ends, to ensure that the load is properly transmitted across the section. A simple flat tie is weakened by the fixing holes at the ends. So such ties are sometimes waisted in the middle, or enlarged at the ends, to achieve a more uniform cross-sectional area throughout the length of the member.

Transom A cross piece, or a lintel.

Triangulation When links are joined by freely adjusted pivots, they form a kinematic chain. With four members, one being fixed, they make a mechanism. If the number of members is reduced to three, they become a rigid frame, or structure. Triangulation is a method of attaining rigidity.

Truss A framed structure, used to support a roof or a bridge. There are several standard designs, e.g. Warren, Pratt.

Valley The hollow between two adjacent ridges. These are usually lined with lead or zinc, to provide a channel for rainwater.

Vaulted Arched or concave construction often seen in ecclesiastical buildings, barns and large halls.

Voussoir A wedge-shaped brick or stone which is a member of an arch.

Warren Girder A girder which, basically, consists of members of equal length, forming a series of equilateral triangles. In the simple cases, the lower horizontal members are ties, and the upper ones struts. These girders can be seen supporting flat or ridged roofing. Some curved girders are built on the same principles.

THE WATCHING SERIES

The aim of the "Watching" series is to draw attention to some of the very interesting items around us, things that perhaps we don't notice as much as we might. *Bridge Watching*, the first of the series, was initially made available "on the Net", where it produced, to the surprise of the author, such a pleasant flood of e-mail that *Water Watching* was subsequently written. This too, was kindly received. The series now contains seven titles, all available in print and e-book formats (e-books available from www.ebrary.com and www.netlibrary.com).

Boat Watching
Edmund W. Jupp

Boats are truly lovely things, from the humblest to the noblest. Given a bit of time, you can lounge against a wall, or a post, or stretch out in a chair, and just drink in the happiness of looking. Looking at things is one of the great free benefits of being alive. You don't have to be an expert, but a little knowledge does help to enjoy the details.

Boat watching doesn't cost anything; it is environmentally friendly; it doesn't call for expensive equipment (you can even do it when there are no boats about, if you have a good imagination).

Paper
1-84150-809-8
£9.95

Bell Watching
Edmund W. Jupp

In England, church bells are well known, because of the sounds they make, though many people have not seen the bells themselves. Doorbells, too, are familiar items in many houses, but are rarely regarded with any particular interest. Some of these are not what is popularly imagined as bell-shaped, and are more properly chimes. Then there are bicycle bells, cowbells, and many other kinds, too, all well worth a thought.

Paper
1-84150-808-X
£9.95

Bridge Watching
Edmund W. Jupp

Wherever we go we seem to meet bridges. Mostly we tend to use them almost without noticing them, except when we see a particularly striking example like the suspension bridge over the river Tamar in Devon. There is no attempt to cover everything about bridges, just enough to make a bridge a more interesting object for you, or your camera, or your paint-box. I do hope it will help you to enjoy bridges, wherever you see them. They are such nice comfortable things to watch, especially when you know something about them.

Paper
1-84150-804-7
£9.95

Brick Watching
Edmund W. Jupp

Armed with a little knowledge, every brick structure is an item of interest, something to be noticed, perhaps to be jotted down in a record, or photographed, drawn, painted, remembered. The author hopes that this gentle approach will provide some insight into the esoteric world of bricks, and will increase the pleasure of finding and studying the many brick structures (including the multitude of fascinating ruins) not only locally but all over the world. It might even convert the reader from being indifferent to becoming enthusiastic.

Paper
1-84150-806-3
£9.95

Roof Watching
Edmund W. Jupp

Roof Watching is an invitation to look at the top covering of buildings! Our eyes are set in our faces so that they look horizontally. Hence, in the ordinary way, people mostly look straight ahead, and don't look up as much as they might. If they did this too much they might not see objects at ground level, and so bump into things, of course; on the other hand, there is a good deal above eye level that is worth seeing. It is not only the outside of a roof that is of interest. Inside there are all sorts of intriguing things. If you hadn't thought much about it before, you may be surprised at what goes on inside the roof space, and what holds it all up. So, inside and outside, the roof is worth some attention, not only when complete, but during its construction, too.

Paper
1-84150-810-1
£9.95

Tunnel Watching
Edmund W. Jupp

Some people find pleasure in taking photographs and some like to sketch or paint, because tunnel mouths are often set in lovely countryside. A train emerging from a hole in the side of a hill makes a good picture, in any weather conditions, whether as a photograph or a painting. On the other hand some people like to just look, without recording the sight. Whichever may be your choice, I wish you happy tunnel-watching. There are other reasons for tunnelling, such as providing an approach for men and materials, to get at something not otherwise accessible from the surface, escaping from a prison, robbing a bank, or following a seam of mineral deposits, perhaps to carry water or other liquids from one place to another.

Paper
1-84150-807-1
£9.95

Water Watching
Edmund W. Jupp

Water watchers enjoy this pleasurable pastime, whatever their educational background; but more knowledge of what to look for will, it is hoped, lead to even more satisfaction. The intention is to encourage interest in looking at water or watery fluids, which are all around us. You don't need any equipment, licences or permits, nor any special qualifications, other than some curiosity and a sense of wonder. The treatment won't be too technical, but hopes to show you how some natural laws control the behaviour and appearance of water. Some knowledge of this can make water so much more fascinating, wherever you see it.

Paper
1-84150-805-5
£9.95

order form

Please send me:

- ❏ Boat Watching
- ❏ Brick Watching
- ❏ Water Watching
- ❏ Bell Watching
- ❏ Roof Watching
- ❏ Bridge Watching
- ❏ Tunnel Watching

Total	
Postage*	
Grand Total	

* Book postage is free in the UK. Please add £2.05 per book for postage elsewhere in the EU and £4.05 per book outside the EU.

⃝ Payment enclosed (Cheques payable to Intellect Ltd.)

⃝ Please charge my Visa / Mastercard No.:

| | | | | | | | | Expiry Date: | | | |

Signature: _____
Name: _____
Address: _____
_____
Postcode: _____
Country: _____ Email: _____

www.intellectbooks.com
email: orders@intellectbooks.com
PO Box 862, Bristol BS99 1DE, UK
Fax: 0117 958 9911